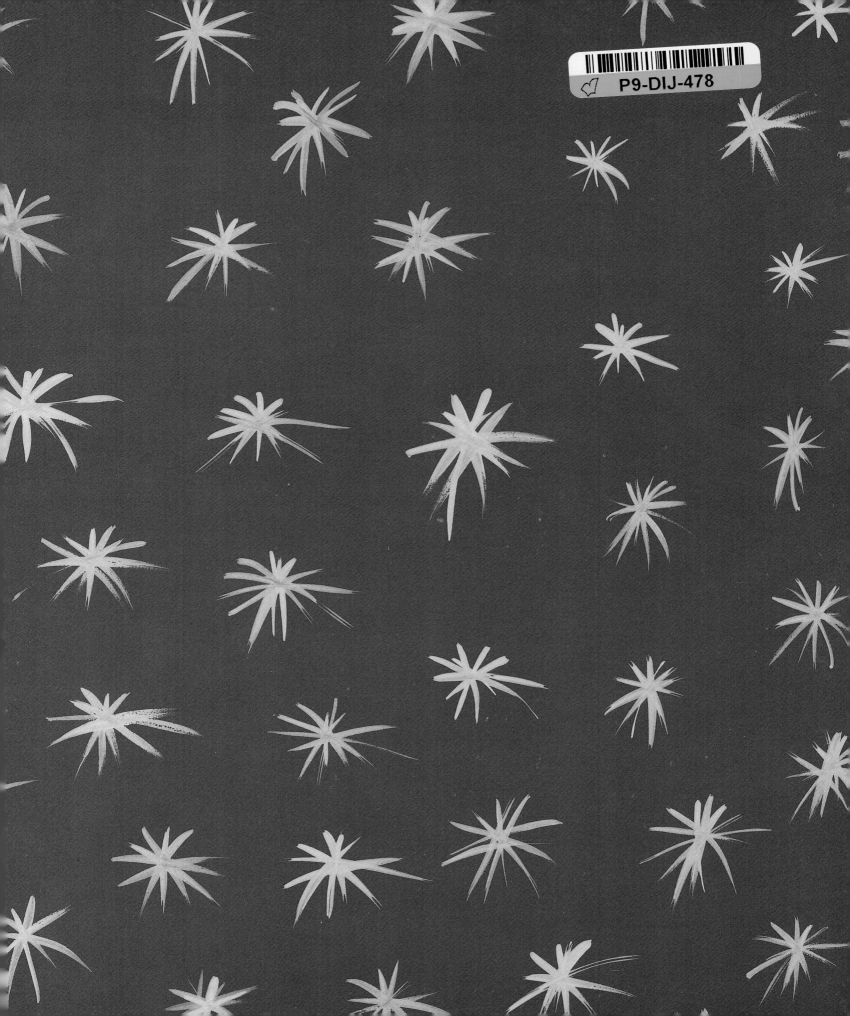

For my parents, whose love I treasure.
—D. G.

Henry Holt and Company, Inc.
Publishers since 1866
115 West 18th Street
New York, New York 10011

Henry Holt is a registered
trademark of Henry Holt and Company, Inc.
Text copyright © 1937 by Macmillan Publishing Company, Inc.
Copyright renewed 1965 by Morgan Guaranty Trust Co. of New York.
Illustrations copyright © 1993 by Dale Gottlieb
All rights reserved.
Published in Canada by Fitzhenry & Whiteside Ltd.,
91 Granton Drive, Richmond Hill, Ontario L4B 2N5.
A CIP catalog record for this book is available.
ISBN 0-8050-2695-9
First Edition—1993
Printed in the United States of America on acid-free paper. ∞
10 9 8 7 6 5 4 3 2 1
The artwork for this book was done in gouache
on Fabriano Artistico 140 lb. paper.

Christmas Carol

A poem by Sara Teasdale
Pictures by Dale Gottlieb

Henry Holt and Company · New York

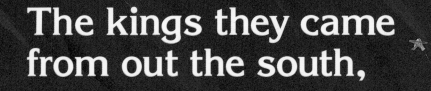

The kings they came
from out the south,

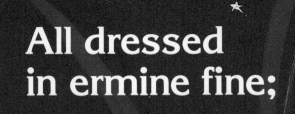

All dressed
in ermine fine;

They bore Him gold
and chrysoprase,

And gifts of
precious wine.

The shepherds came from out the north,

Their coats were brown and old;

They brought Him little
newborn lambs—

They had not any gold.

The wise men came from out the east,

And they were wrapped in white;

The star that led them all the way

Did glorify the night.

The angels came from heaven high,

And they were clad with wings;

And lo, they brought a joyful song

The host of heaven sings.

The kings they knocked upon the door,
The wise men entered in,

The shepherds followed
after them
To hear the song begin.

The angels sang through
all the night
Until the rising sun,

But little Jesus fell asleep
Before the song was done.